Finding Money,
over 500 places to find spare cash in your life.

By J. Godsey

SicPress 2012
METHUEN, MA

TABLE OF CONTENTS

PREFACE TO THE SECOND EDITION.

Thank you to the three hundred people who purchased digital copies of the previous edition of Finding Money. And thank you to all the people who contributed their advice so generously to the earlier book.

So much has changed since the first edition was cobbled together as fundraising item for ARMV. The changes in the second edition should be obvious, the ideas are more finely sorted, and the blatant duplications have been compressed. Many ideas that won't work in the new economy have been replaced with newer ideas. Still I hope you will find a few ideas in this edition that will help you find a few extra dollars that you hadn't realized before.

Everyone who writes a self help book has advice on how YOU should change your life to be more like theirs. Obviously, you are doing something wrong otherwise yours would be perfect, like theirs; and you wouldn't need a ride or a job or a loan. Sometimes we just need to raid the couch cushions of our life, because we can't pay a utility bill, because we lost our income, or part of our income.

Finding Money is a little unusual compared to similar frugal advice books, it is a book filled with smacks on the side of the head. It contains multiple and sometimes contradictory suggestions; because there is no ONE way to live. What works for one person may not work for another. Where one person can cut back, another can eliminate altogether. I am not promising to solve your monetary woes or even make a dent in them, but I can say that somewhere in here is ONE suggestion that will make this book pay for itself. That's all you need to get you started.

Everything here is optional. It all depends on what you are ready to do personally. Inside I have collected large and obvious ways to save money and a lot of tiny ways you can squeeze out a few extra pennies. Many, many of them I use myself. It may not seem to add up to much, but sometimes pinching a few pennies here and there, can keep us going until things get better.

I hope this helps you just a little bit.

As with all my little books, profits from the sale of this book go to animal rescue.

J. GODSEY

PERSONAL

Stay healthy – being sick is expensive

Stay legal – lawyers and court costs are expensive

Stay safe – being injured is expensive

Learn a new skill – increases your flexibility in job market and around the home

Take classes online – the more talents you have on your resume the better you look, online learning is cheaper and endlessly available.

Move in with your parents – or rather have them move in with you; multi-generational households are more efficient than separate living arrangements.

Move if you have to – do the math, some places costs less to live than others, some places have better job prospects; save money with a smaller apartment or in a less desirable community.

Sell or rent out your house – Move to an apartment of condo which will cut down on outdoor responsibilities and be more energy efficient.

Get a roommate – if you have a spare room and can find someone you can stand, this is a great way to split expenses.

Telecommute – if you are mostly doing desk work, see what portion can be done at home.

Don't spend – See how many days you can go without spending money. Plan to have no spend weekends.

Save your pocket change, don't count it, just bring it to the bank when you go and put it in your savings account.

FRIENDS AND FAMILY

Agree to limit gift giving – many families would love to limit group gifting to a certain amount, limit it to handmade or even eliminate it, but no one wants to be first to suggest it. Get together with ONE other person and present it together.

Shop early. – Start holiday shopping in September buying items when they appear on clearance making room for holiday items. Try to be done before Black Friday.

Give homemade gifts – soaps, breads, candles and such make appropriate housewarming, thank-yous and other casual gifts, such as handmade only, are great for reducing costs.

Avoid friends with lavish lifestyles – these friends may influence you to keep up with their spending habits, regardless of whether they are over extended or flush; it will only make you feel inferior.

Donate time, instead of money – Charities still need money more than ever, but if you can donate time, they can use that too.

Eliminate greeting cards – make a phone call, or hand write a note, much cheaper and more personal. Greeting cards that must be bought can be purchased at a dollar store and personalized with your own words.

Send post cards. – they cost half as much to mail; you can cut holiday cards in half and use them as post cards

Volunteer your free time – keeps you busy, opens you up to social networking, enlarges your contact with potential employers, customers, and opportunities.

Have home pot-lucks with your friends – in lieu of eating out or throwing dinner parties.

Learn how to mix drinks at home – hand made craft cocktails with friends will taste infinitely better and be much cheaper than the ones at your local pub.

Troll the marked down toy aisle and store a few discounted 'gift' toys for upcoming mandatory gift events.

CLOTHING

Don't buy trendy clothing – the fashion will change and you won't get as many years out of it; it is usually poorly made as well.

Don't buy cheap clothes – when buying either new or used, cheap clothes will not last and takes more effort to care for. Learn how to tell the difference between well made clothing and the other kind. Good clothing in classic styles last for many years, decades even generations.

Take care of your clothing – wash them properly and not too often that they become faded, fix small tears before they become large ones.

Wash your clothes less frequently – over washing leads to wear, if you are clean, your clothes should last a few wearings before they need it.

Avoid dry cleaning – a wrinkle releasing spray and a fabric refresher can make something last a little longer before having to be dry cleaned.

Used clothing: buying. – Avoid buying 'new' new clothes unless you can't avoid it – many items in thrift shop have never been worn, and others are just as good as new. If you look for Quality made items or high-end labels, you will get great deals.

Used clothing: selling. – When buying used, don't just look for items for yourself, look for items you can resell online. Name brand items do very well online, since the quality is known and the sizes can be verified.

Learn to Sew. – The cost of a local sewing class is easily offset with a few projects. besides fixing clothing, make Pillowcases from old sheets, trim worn bath towels into hand towels buy adding a hem. Make simple gift items.

Get a sewing machine. – A basic name brand machine isn't very much, but you have to know that you will use it to make the cost back, so try one out first. Freecycle or craigslist are your best bet for a discount. Borrow a sewing machine, or go halves with one with a family member or good friend.

Alter your clothing – before throwing or donating something out of style, try your hand at altering it, either yourself or use a tailor for better clothes. There are tons of how to videos on Youtube on every aspect of sewing.

Learn to knit. – Making gifts and house hold items is cheaper. You can also trade or sell your items.

Hemming party. – if you have a sewing machine or borrow one, announce that you will be having a hemming weekend or party. have friends and family bring their TO be hemmed items over and do them while they wait.

Reading Material

Eliminate the newspaper - if you only read the Sunday paper, cancel the rest of the week.

Taste test books from the library - even if you know you want to buy it, check it out from the library first to be certain; more often then not you will find you don't need to own it.

Dust off your library card - libraries have books, audio books, DVDs, CDs, magazines and newspapers

Cancel your magazines - many magazines can be borrowed from the library, magazines have much of their material online; or split the cost with a friend.

Viewing Material

Cancel cable TV. Roku streaming devices help you access lots of free streaming channels off the internet. cut back to basic cable and watch things online or on DVD; Hulu.com, Netflix, Instant Watch, Amazon Prime.

Buy an online membership to stream movies - Netflix.com and Amazon Prime have unlimited streaming. Roku Streaming player opens up many channels with free viewing.

Watch things for free on the internet - many public domain items are watchable for free at archive.org, Hulu.com, and Youtube. FreeDocumentaries.org has many documentaries put online by their creators.

ENTERTAINMENT

Invite friends over instead of going out - even if it is pot-luck or pizza, an evening of friends and playing games at home is cheaper than dinner and drinks elsewhere

Recreate locally - check out what your town has for greenspaces and sporting venues, saves time and gas and usually money.

Take up running, cycling or hiking - These sports take very little investment for the amount of satisfaction.

Look for annual passes - museums or zoos, etc. local libraries usually have them to check out for free.

Attend semi-pro, college or high school sports - these tickets are much easier to get than professional sports tickets and the experience can be more satisfying.

Matinees for movies and plays save money. - Check your local venues online at Fandango.com find the cheapest movie tickets.

Don't buy food in theaters - this should be obvious, you can go two hours without a snack, if you can't just put a bag of raisins or M&Ms in your pocket.

Don't gamble - unless you are a professional and have the requisite skills to do it for a living, don't bother. You will make more money putting away each dollar you would have spent on a lottery ticket, than you will win ever from the lottery.

EATING IN

Eat breakfast – this will keep you from snacking throughout the morning and energize you early.

Eat lunch – this will keep you from nodding off and snacking through the rest of the day.

Drink tap water – fill your bottle from the tap, if your town's water 'really' has a flavor buy a filter for it. You can buy powdered add in flavorings for your water, some sugar free, which can make it tastier; a shot of fruit juice works just as well.

Tea and Toast. Eat one major meal a day, and a light meal and make another one tea and toast or crackers and cheese, something filling that will fill you up until your next meal.

Crackers do matter – keep good lightly salted unsweetened crackers in the house – a few of these and a cup of tea can keep one from raiding the fridge and make a quick dinner when combined with very good cheese.

Bottle your own water – use a filter or buy spring water by the gallon and a reusable bottle.

Bring a thermos – make great coffee at home and bring it with you, even if you buy really great beans, it will be cheaper than buying it out.

Bring your lunch – nearly anything you bring from home is better and cheaper than eating out. Splurge and make your favorite things: sushi, roast beef, crepes, make your coworkers jealous; but eat out with your coworkers every so often so they don't think you are too cheap.

Don't drink soda pop or energy drinks – keeps you healthier and avoids empty calories. soda is basically carbonated water with high fructose corn syrup added.

Eat better – don't buy cheap calories, junk food, sugar cereals, and unhealthy foods. Better food will fill you up and your body will process the nutrition efficiently. Cheap calories only make you think you are full and your body will want more nutrition.

Eat less – go on a diet.

Give up sugar cereal – hot cereals are healthier and way cheaper.

Eat less meat – meat is very expensive to produce and healthier cuts are very expensive to purchase.

Eat more vegetables – become vegetarian if you can, weekday vegetarianism is becoming more common.

Eat Asian cuisine – Asian cuisines are low in meat content and high in vegetables and rice.

Pretend Restaurant – Cooking your favorite dishes and trying a new recipe now and then is much cheaper than eating out, and can make a pretty good substitute for a restaurant meal.

EATING OUT

Don't do it. That is impractical advice but basic. If you are a couple or a family, try cutting back to once a month so it becomes an occasion you plan for and savor.

Carry snacks – this will keep you from buying some during the day.

Don't eat out alone – the service is rarely good.

Get on mailing lists for local restaurants and vendors – their emails and newsletters will contain discounts and coupons just for members.

Buy an entertainment coupon book – but only if you are going to use enough coupons to cover the cost at least three times over; otherwise leave your money in your pocket.

Don't eat out on weekends – most restaurants have their best specials during the week to encourage customers, the service is usually better on quite nights anyway.

Go for lunch specials – many restaurants have their dinner items on special for lunch

Don't order an entree – an appetizer and/or a side dish is usually plenty for one person.

Skip dessert – if you want dessert at that restaurant, skip the appetizer or have just a side for your meal

Split the entrée – if you know a restaurant serves 'way too much' split the entree with your partner

Drink water with your meal – saves money and helps you digest your food, also improves the flavor.

Get two meals out of one – if you know a restaurant serves 'way too much', eat the sides and save half the entree for your meal or lunch the next day.

HEALTH

Don't smoke – saves boat loads of money and keeps you healthy, also improves your hirability and insurability.

Don't drink or cut back – this saves boat loads of money. Alcoholic drinks are empty calories, the markup in bars is tremendous.

Buy generic medications when you can - they are usually exactly the same as their brand named versions and cost less.

Cancel health club membership - walk, run, cycle, work, garden, these are all good antidotes to our sedentary lifestyles.

Cut back your hobbies to one - too many hobbies are waste time and money, drop all but the one you love the most, but don't drop all of them, you need it to stay sane.

Cut your hair - long hair costs more to maintain, tag team with a friend to cut each other's hair. Do it less frequently than normal, try a different style that will stay in style longer.

Grow you hair - getting your hair cut every few months costs money

Dilute your shampoo - shampoos and conditioners are sold stronger than they have to be; diluted product will disperse in your hair quicker and easier.

Put your shampoo in pump bottle - this will cut way back on how much you use.

Get your hair cut at a school - look for a hair styling school in your area; don't forget to check the vocational schools.

Get your glasses replaced or repaired online - all you need is your prescription to buy new glasses or have new frames for your lenses.

Use a dental school- look for a dental school and look into having students work on your teeth

Have your doctor write you a three month prescription - then you only pay one co-pay instead of three.

Use a pill splitter – ask your doctor if he can prescribe pills that are twice the dosage and cut them in half to make twice as many pills, leaving you with only one co-pay instead of two.

Use washable menstrual pads and menstrual cups – thirty or forty years of disposable feminine products adds up to a lot of money.

FOOD SHOPPING

Bring a calculator – or use the one in your phone, keep track of your shopping total, it creeps up fast.

Make a shopping list – when you go out for errands use the list to estimate and limit your spending, but don't be rigid, if you see something on sale, take advantage of it.

Do the MATH. Sometimes large containers are cheaper per unit price, sometimes the sale on the median 15 oz size is better. Usually the smaller container costs a lot more that the other sizes; but if it's something you won't finish anyway, just buy the small one.

Don't rationalize shopping – if you don't need it, don't buy it. Figure out what will happen to the item when you don't want it anymore.

Don't shop for fun – not even window shopping, avoid impulse buying.

Don't shop hungry – this will put pressure on you to impulse buy.

Play games – challenge yourself to get all your groceries into four bags, or under $50 dollars, see what has the best nutritional value in the store for the least amount of money.

Do food shopping once a month - track your use and shop once a month, avoid shopping until that day.

Look for discounted meats - depending on the overall trust-worthiness of the meat department, manager's specials on meat are usually great deals.

Get a membership in community supported agriculture - farm memberships are a much cheaper way to buy vegetables. You may have to save up for a season to pay for it the first time, but it will be easier after you start saving on your purchases.

Have a grocery budget - when you are shopping have a number in mind $20, $50, $100 and stop when you get to it, put back things that can wait until next time.

Join a food co-op - this spreads the overhead costs amongst all the members.

Use reusable grocery bags - many stores give credit or charges fees to encourage this.

Don't use disposable products - paper plates, utensils, napkins, things that have only one use in them are wasted money.

Don't buy sale items you don't use - just because it's on sale, doesn't mean you need it.

Do the math when buying bulk - you may retail warehouse stores aren't always cheaper, find restaurant supply houses on the other hand which often are cheaper.

Check expiration dates on everything - even packaged groceries; cookies and crackers have expiration dates, imported items are notorious for being expired and still on the shelf. Expiration dates may be generous but if you aren't going to eat it right away, you may forget it in the cupboard.

Don't buy special items that you don't eat that often. Limit the food stuffs that you buy to a certain rotation that you cook and eat on a regular basis. That jar you opened once will sit in the back of the fridge until you throw it.

Shop at ethnic grocery stores - these may have better prices on those cuisine items, such as rice, dried vegetables, bulk spices etc

Shop the outer edges of the grocery store - this is where the 'fresh' non processed foods are found.

Split a large meat order - when buying a side of beef straight from the farm, you can save by going in with other people/families.

Buy items in bulk that you consume on a regular basis. If Kidney beans are on sale, buy them and store them, canned or dried they last forever.

Buy large cuts or meat - cut a large roast into smaller ones, cut chickens in to pieces it is not hard and if you screw it up the first time you can still cook it. Check out the how to videos on Youtube.com, and find Julia Child's videos. Avoid items that are heavily advertised - the costs of the advertising is worked into the price of the item.

Avoid processed food - foods that have been precut, shredded, processed, cooked or treated cost more. Pre cut boiled potatoes in a bag cost more than 10 pounds of raw potatoes. Shredded cheese costs a lot more than block cheese and a cheese grated combined.

Avoid products that are heavily couponed –items that have coupons issued on a regular basis are overpriced.

Buy food in season - things are cheaper in season.

Buy local - items that don't have to been shipped may cost less, eggs from a local farm will be better and cheaper. Check your state's agricultural websites and look for local farmers and producers.

Choose the cheapest store – do the bulk of your shopping at the store that is cheapest over all, and only go to the more expensive store for unique items. Start at the dollar store or the discount store and buy what you can, then take the rest of the list to the major supermarket.

Shop elsewhere. – You can find discount luxuries for gifts – high-end chocolates, teas, jams and cookies can be found marked down drastically at discount department stores. Breakfast cereals are more drastically discounted at Pharmacy chains than at supermarkets, their two for one sale is a loss leader.

Ship Amazon.com – not as a regular course. But check the prices of everything you eat on a regular basis. Sometimes you CAN make out on the large quantity items with the free shipping. Especially if it is something you really like , such as a particular brand of tea, and you won't be buying something 'instead' at the store because you can't find what you want.

Customer cards – Customer cards can save you money. If you can get away without carrying a card, just have them look you up by phone number, then you won't forget your card or decide which customer cards are taking up too much room, photocopy the bar codes, put them all on one card and put THAT card back in your wallet instead.

Plan which toys to buy ahead of time and have it delivered – avoiding the toy store saves time, money, and aggravation and avoids impulse buying.

Shop a discount club – these are much better places to get office supplies, than most office supply stores; small business memberships can actually have an annual return on your shopping.

Sign up free customer rewards programs – create a Gmail address just to use for these and other junk mail producing programs.

FOOD STORAGE

Date your consumables – when you put away groceries, mark them with the date, a few months of this will help you track your usage and plan your future shopping.

Get a freezer – try Freecycle.com or Craigslist.com, use it for bulk purchases and bulk meal cooking. A lot of people have them sitting around from when THEY had to save money. Don't PAY for one more than a few years old. Put that money towards a new one, even a new energy efficient one will make it's money back saving power. The older ones won't be cost effective unless they are free.

Fill the freezer – If the freezer is less than half filled, add milk bottles filled with water. Freezers are more efficient when they are filled.

Invest in some reusable freezer containers – whatever single serving size you are most likely to use. Start with one or two and see if they are convenient. Then you can freeze leftovers in exactly the right quantity for defrosting.

Reuse zipper sandwich and freezer bags – but not more than once or twice. They aren't designed that way.

Watch the fan/vent – keep fan and vents clear for air circulation in the freezer.

Donate or eat the odd foodstuffs from the back of the cupboard before they go bad. You want that room to store food you are actually meal planning around.

Start a stockpile - Not necessarily the huge voluminous extreme couponing piles, but just a cupboard of extra items bought on sale on in bulk. Stock piles aren't just for disasters, if you have a week or a months worth of food you can dip into it to tide you over when you run out of food money. Don't forget to fill it up again. Think of it like your own food bank.

COOKING

Learn to cook. You don't have to be a chef to cook properly. Learn BASIC techniques and recipes and knife skills. Youtube and other websites are chock full of instructional videos on these skills.

Bake Bread. Baking one loaf of bread a week, saves at least $2 on a store bought loaf of bread. Bake two put one in the freezer or trade them to a neighbor for eggs or jam etc. Cheap bread isn't worth eating and healthy store bought bread is expensive.

Do the math on new recipes - a yummy recipe from a magazine sounds great, until you add up what it costs to buy the ingredients, you may as well have gone out to dinner; if you have to buy a condiment just for the one recipe it may not be worth it.

Cook something from scratch every week. Very few of us have time to cook all our meals from scratch, but if you cook spaghetti sauce on Sunday in a crock pot you have spaghetti sauce for various meals during the week or to add to the freezer.

Trade meals with someone else - each cook a different meal and split it between you both.

Make cookies and treats – do this on the weekend and you have snacks for all week, cook once a month and freeze them for later.

Create your own low calorie servings – take bulk purchased items and divide them into reusable bags by serving, then you know how much you are consuming.

Avoid heating your oven for small amounts – ovens take a lot of energy to heat up and stay at a constant temperature.

Cook turkey and roasts inside cooking bags – aside from keeping it moist, this will eliminate much of the clean up saving money on oven cleaner and utensils; oven cleaner is more expensive than bulk bought bags.

Cook in batches and freeze individually having ready-made meals in the freezer saves energy and time to thaw small portions.

Cook smaller meals – avoids waste.

Save leftover vegetables – keep a two-quart container in the freezer and when it's more than half full, make soup or stock.

Extend the life of milk by heating it – when it just becomes expired, you can stop the process with heat: make café au lait, hot chocolate, or chai tea.

Make your own baby food in a food processor – make it at the same time you make your dinner, it will be healthier

Make your own stock – it costs pennies to throw a chicken carcass and some vegetables in water; you rend every bit of flavor and protein out of it.

Develop a repertoire of meals, if you cook the same two or three dozen recipes, you can predict what you need to have on hand.

Use smaller counter top or toaster ovens – they heat quickly and cool fast, and only heat the food item instead of an empty space around the food.

Use a pressure cooker – these speeding up cooking and retaining moisture. Great item to find on Freecycle, keep an eye on the rubber gaskets and replace when they get brittle.

Use a slow cooker – these are more energy efficient for items that take time to cook, meats, root vegetables and beans. Newer ones run higher wattage than older ones, older ones can be found at thrift stores and yard sales. Think about running two if you intend to freeze meals.

COUPONING

Visit couponing websites – many product coupons are available to download, create a separate email for these accounts to keep the spam emails at bay.

Track prices of your most used items – find the vendor with the best price, and the time of year it goes on sale.

Look for online ebates, rebates and coupons before you shop – working these in combination with a sale can save money on a purchase

Keep a price index – if you buy items repeatedly keep track of the costs at various stores you may find they go on sale on a regular basis.

Keep a coupon file, one doesn't need to be a super coupon user to benefit from coupons. Just cutting them and having them when shopping makes a profit.

Send away for manufacturer's coupons – many large companies send these out on request or if you send in a complaint, sometimes you can do this on their website.

Use coupon clipping services, if you know you will be buying a lot of something, these folks can save you quite a bit

Shop alone – this will eliminate discussion and save time, it will also eliminate someone else's impulse buying and distraction from your shopping plans.

Write to manufacturers – Once a year write to each major maker of your food products, either a complaint or a compliment or better yet both. Nearly will send you free coupons and they are always better than any you get from other sources.

Write for free samples – don't just hit websites and send emails. Major consumer oriented companies pay more attention to actual MAIL.

Non-Food

Join your local Freecycle.com groups – usually the one for your town and any abutting towns is plenty; ask there first before buying things.

Avoid brand name items – unless there is no substitute, most items with a 'name' brand are overpriced as you are paying for their advertising on top of the item's cost

Avoid department stores – if you don't go into big box stores you won't be tempted to buy things you don't need.

Avoid paying for extras – Buy the basic model of the device, if a device does extraordinary things and you never use it, that is a wasted investment. A toaster is a toaster, a toaster that fries an egg is silly.

Buy the simplest device you can get away with – buy mechanical instead of electronic, buy analog instead of digital. You may save money on the electricity, or maintenance. Analog devices can usually BE repaired, digital devices not so much.

Avoid buying the newest gadgets and devices – if the one you have is still working, don't look to replace it until it breaks. New items don't work that much better than the last version, and if it is a completely new device, later models will work more consistently.

Don't buy extended warranties – these are usually on items where it is cheaper to replace the item

Decide between need and want – wants can be transitory, you may want something today, but not have much use for it tomorrow.

Buy second hand when you can – books,DVDs, CDs, bicycles, tools and other hard goods are all cheaper on the secondary market.

Buy individual items online – saves driving to multiple stores looking for that one item. If you know exactly what item you need and you aren't sure where you can find it many websites have free shipping, Amazon does for over $25 purchases. You can save a lot of gas money ordering online.

Cut down or eliminate paper products – it may be cheaper to use dishtowels instead or paper towels and napkins; buy them in bulk from a restaurant supply house or second hand at yard sales

Buy or try generic cleaning products – for the most part brand name cleaning products are indistinguishable from generics. Concentrated generics are very cheap to use. Powdered are even cheaper, look for them in hardware and paint stores.

Buy cleaning supplies in bulk – they are cheaper at janitorial, restaurant and industrial suppliers, even large hardware stores.

Bleach, Ammonia, Vinegar, Baking soda, washing soda (Sodium carbonate) are all perfectly good cleansers. Beware certain combinations but if it was good enough to clean your grandmother's house, how much dirtier is yours?

Look for online coupon codes - sites like RetailMeNot.com have active coupon codes which you can use online at many sites.

Look for concentrated cleaning products - the ready made store bought items are mostly water, the denser the original purchase the lower the cost. Powdered detergents can still be found in hardware stores and paint stores.

Use elbow grease, Magic Erasers and green scrub pads bought in bulk can save detergent by cleaning without much at all. Generic eraser sponges are available on eBay.

Make your purchases wait in the car - if you do buy something you don't need immediately, leave it in the car with the receipt for a few days. If you still need it, bring it in, otherwise return it.

Optimize yard sales - don't buy things you don't need because they are a 'good buy' unless you intend to sell it or give it away. Don't be afraid to haggle, come back at the end of the day and look for freebies.

Start a product review website - if you like a particular kind of product a reviewing website will attract companies who mail samples, the more narrow the focus the better.

Take advantage of loss leaders - regardless of whether and item is on your shopping list, if an item you use is on sale, stock up on it, even if you have to store the excess under the bed.

Take advantage of yearly sales – certain things go on sale once a year, most often after Christmas and before spring

BABY

Buy second hand baby clothing – they grow out of them very quickly

Borrow baby furniture – or buy second hand, the odds are you will only use it for a year or two.

Get furniture and accessories that do double duty. Cribs can be transformed into toddler bed, high chairs that transform into booster seats. Our parents bought very little special furniture.

Buy gender neutral baby clothes – this will allow fore re-use regardless of sex.

Don't buy baby clothes far in advance – Newborns can have sudden growth spurts,

Lose the shoes – babies will learn to walk faster if they're barefoot when they're indoors. Use soft booties to keep feet warm when you're outside.

Buy secondhand special-occasion clothes – from the consignment shop fraction of its retail cost. Chances are its previous owner wore the princess dress or suit just once or twice.

Return unwanted gifts promptly. Merchants often put time limits on returns and exchanges; you don't want to miss your chance.

Set up a photo Website instead of printing – post your baby pics online for free at some sites Friends and relatives can then print out their own copies.

Think big about diapers. - Lugging home one of those 228-count cartons from the wholesale club will save about $170 a year.

Try the generic diapers - considering the price differential they are worth trying. They are only going to end up in a landfill anyway.

Watch the pricing - the larger they are the fewer there are in the package.

Buy by the case. - If you buy by the case, tape the receipt to the box. If you child outgrows that size before you open it, exchange it for the next size up.

Store brand formula - by law the store brand and the name brand must have the same nutritional value. Choose powder over liquid, you are only paying for the water.

Check your library for classes and games.- There's a waiting list for the story times and activities and events at my library. They also have wooden puzzles and other toys to play with.

Keep a back up baby bag in the car - In case you lose or forget your regular baby bag. Make sure it contains three diapers, a tube of ointment, a travel pack of wipes, an extra outfit, and, if your child eats solid foods, a small snack like a teething biscuit or some vegetable puffs. You can also raid it when run out of any one thing.

FIX THINGS

Fix it. - The rule of thumb is that if it would cost 50% of less than the replacement cost, then it is worth fixing rather than replacing.

Learn your tools. - Collect them in one place, keep them clean and stored safely. Rusty tools don't work well. Throw broken tools away.

Buy tools one at a time. - Don't buy a special tool until you need it, a pipe wrench isn't something you need until you are ready to use it.

Learn how to fix things. - Another trip to Youtube, eHow.com, DoItYourself.com, and Instructables.com to learn how to solve individual problems. You will be surprised how easy it is to fix a knob. Sugru.com self curing silicon is one of the new materials out there for fixing things instead of replacing them.

Borrow or rent tools - if you only need something once or twice try borrow or renting it.

Assemble a 'fix it' tool box or drawer using the items in your junk drawer. superglue, duct tape, wire, glue gun, liquid nail, hot glue gun, magnets, shower curtain hooks, bungee cords, industrial strength velcro etc...

Learn to maintain and repair your appliances - find and download your manuals, avoids replacement, and maintains efficiency.

Find parts online. Replace broken or missing parts by finding the part number on the item or online. Usually the manufacturer's site will have old manuals and part numbers. Email them if they don't. If they don't sell the replacement part, Google it as there are replacement part companies, even some that sell used parts.

Print a part. If the part you need is no longer made and impossible to find, there are 3 printing services online, where you can send the part for scanning and they can make a replacement. It may be costly but it also may be cheaper than buying a new washing machine or other device.

CLIMATE CONTROL

Turn down water heater thermostat.

Close unused rooms – to save heat or a/c close off unused rooms.

Add more insulation – blown in the walls, layered in the attic, check the loss around the windows.

Wear a sweater and socks – just because you're cold doesn't mean the heat needs to be turned up, put on one or two pairs of socks, and a sweater and undershirt, generations of English people can't be wrong; work in bed if you can.

Add solar panels – if you can add even one solar panel to charge one battery item you are saving energy you don't have to pay for. You can get small ones that attach to your window and charge household batteries and items

Avoid turning on the air conditioning – turn the ac on for short times usually in the early am or evenings to cool the area down, then turn it off until the next time it is needed.

Change the filters in air conditioners and furnaces – keep systems running at optimum Efficiency

Close your blinds and curtains to keep temperatures down – this will block some heat from the sun.

Open your blinds and curtains in the winter – let the sun heat some of your house.

Place window air conditioners on the shadiest side of the house – if possible, it will be easier for it to work, plant a shade tree nearby, put an awning over it.

Check your storm windows – sometimes they become loose over time and need to be sealed or repaired.

Install a door sweep - this will cover the gap under the front door.

Seal the electric outlets - install foam seals inside the outlet covers.

Seal your windows for the winter - using removable silicon sealant, leave the unused windows sealed the rest of the year.

Shut vents in unused rooms - unless you have forced air heating this can save on your heating and cooling bill.

Work outside - if it is too hot to work in the house, don't; take your work outside, run a power cord or ethernet cable if you have to.

Wrap your water heater / pipes - insulating your hot water heater and pipes saves energy

Turn your thermostat down in winter and keep it there - avoid fluctuations in temperature, put on a sweater when cold, use a space heater to warm your space.

Turn your thermostat down when you leave the house or sleep - when you aren't using it, conserve it

Unblock baseboards and heat exchanges - keep these places clear for radiant heat efficiency.

Use a programmable thermostat - this can turn your heat off or low when you are not at home or asleep.

Use fans to move heat - move the fans to distribute the heat where it is needed.

Block up your fireplace - cut a piece of foam insulation to fit inside the flue; this will keep drafts and keep your heat inside your home.

ELECTRICITY

Replace incandescent bulbs with energy efficient bulbs – use the compact fluorescent bulbs or ideally LED.

Reserve rechargeable batteries for high use items – these are rarely cost effective on items you don't use often, like a portable radio, but they work out well for things such as cameras.

Be ruthless about excess lighting – if you aren't in a room turn off the lights, if you are in a room only turn on what you need. Remove bulbs and lamps from the area to prevent casual overuse,

Pretend power outage – one night a week or a month turn everything off and use candles and lamps for the evening, have a candle lighted dinner, tell ghost stories, read a book by lamplight.

Buy a smaller fridge- if you are one person you may not need a family size fridge, selling it and buying a smaller one may save money.

Check the temperature inside your fridge – make sure it is set at the ideal level to keep cold without freezing or spoiling.

Clean behind the refrigerator – improves energy efficiency.

Only run your dishwasher when full – or not at all, consider selling it on craigslist.

Only use half your normal dishwasher detergent – you already prewashed the dishes right?

Turn off the dishwasher after the rinse cycle – let the dishes drip dry.

Use timers on your lamps and devices, or on power strips – if it is blinking or has a red light when not it in use, it

33

is ON; easy-on features for televisions and devices keep the machines powered at a low level when 'off'.

Sweep instead of using the vacuum – sweep more often and save the vacuum for once a week or longer; buy a more efficient broom.

Take care of children's clothing – pre-treat stains and wash special outfits in cold water to minimize fading. You can resell kids clothes when out grown.

WATER

Turn off the water while brushing – do you really need that going?

Install efficiency toilets – upgrading from very old model toilets may save you enough money on your water bill to justify the expense.

Simulate a new low flow toilet – instead of installing a new, water-saver toilet you can displace some water so that less is used each time you flush, with a plastic jug filled with pebbles or a brick wrapped in a plastic bag; add a new more efficient float cap valve assembly before the ancient one breaks; check all the seals.

Reroute the spent water from the sink – and use it to flush the toilet or water the garden.

Install a toilet tank sink – these are becoming easier to find and less peculiar. The water to wash your fingers goes into the tank to flush the toilet.

Install faucet aerators – uses less water.

Install low flow shower heads – a simple item that saves water.

Install a tankless water heater – which only heats the water when you call for it.

Check the temperature of the water heater - , and run it as low as you dare.

Cold water - Turn it off all together in the summer time.

Add a smidgen of toilet bowl cleaner ever night or every other night, the bowl stays clean and you won't have to scrub it.

Wash with a cloth - skip a shower and wash with a washcloth, your mother and grandmother did it.

Take showers not baths- this saves a lot of energy heating the water

Shower with a friend - this definitely saves water and is a lot more fun.

LAUNDRY

Clean the dryer lint trap - do it every time you use it, it is a fire hazard if you don't.

Cut drier sheets in half - they do make a difference with sheets and towels, but you only need a little bit.

Hang your clothes outside - or inside or in a spare room; every load not run through the drier saves a little more.

Stop ironing - Add a smidgen of fabric softener to the rinse, or put a dryer sheet in the dryer for the 1st few minutes. Then take the damp clothes out, shake them and hang them. They will dry without wrinkles.

Only wash in cold water. - if you are using detergent in a new machine you don't need hot water.

Buy Vinegar - Available in gallons in every supermarket. Vinegar will help get the excess soap out of your clothes, as well as substitute for fabric softener in the rinse.

Keep your appliances clean - this will make them last longer. Do an empty wash load with either bleach of vinegar every so often.

Laundry sharing - if you only do small loads of laundry, split the costs with a friend.

Only run full loads of laundry, hand wash what needs to be done immediately.

Use a spot treating product - especially while away from home, like Tide on the Go, keeps stains and spots from sinking in.

Pretreat - use a spray product on grease and stains before you put the clothing into the laundry basket. Then it will work at the stain while it is waiting to be washed.

Use cloth diapers - don't be so dainty, you don't need a service; disposables are helpful when you are away from home, but are still not necessary.

Use cold water for laundry - reserve hot water loads for those that really need it.

Use less laundry detergent - too much soap isn't just a waste of money, it gunks up your machine, can cause mold growth inside your washer, and shortens the life of the appliance; modern dishwashers and washing machines are designed to use much less water and detergent than their predecessors, but we still use what our mother showed us.

COMMUNICATION & DATA

Avoid roaming charges - check your cell service program, make sure it is optimal for your habits.

Call off peak - if you a have a peak time service, use it and save your calling for nights and weekends.

Combine media services - companies that combine cable, phone and internet services offer discounts.

Consider prepaid cell phone - depending on how few minutes you use, you may do better with a prepaid cell phone.

Don't add cell phone extras - no special rings, no games no applications.

Don't text - unless you get unlimited texting with your account, it may not be worth the cost of the service.

Monitor your cell phone minutes - this can usually be done with a #number, overcharges are much more expensive then regular minutes

Optimize your internet plan - if you are a casual user check to see if there is a slower service you could be using.

Optimize your phone bill - periodically check to see if you are on the most efficient program for your calling usage.

Remove your land line - go to cell phone only

Utilize in-network calling - mobile to mobile, in-network, Favorites, or whatever your carrier calls it this week.

Use free directory assistance when on your cell phone - try using Free411 by calling 1-800-free411.

Use a VOIP telephone service - infinitely cheaper than cell and land lines; Skype.com

DEVICES

Buy refilled ink and toner - either use refilling kits or simple buy them already refilled, this will save you at least half the cost of new ones

Buy refurbished equipment – find a local repair service that refurbishes and sells equipment, they will always offer a warranty on their work.

Replace real fax machine and dedicated line with online faxing service, it saves paper, toner and landline charges. There are free services and pay services, even the pay services are cheaper than having a landline or buying supplies.

Do the math on rebates – it may not be worth the time and trouble to submit rebates for small amounts, larger rebates may be worth it if the item is already on sale; buying an item at full retail with the promise of a rebate is not as good as buying a different item on sale.

Clean the fans on the hard drive- cuts back on servicing the machine

Delay purchasing – don't buy something until it will costs you money not to have it. If you impose a waiting period you may find you didn't need the item after all or that the price has gone down.

Keep your computer clean – don't keep excess software or files on your computer, off load images and music to a spare hard drive – avoid loading junk software, this will keep your machine running as it should.

Shop for shipping – compare shipping costs on your items, the USPS is often the most economical, and the flat rate can be the better service; shipgooder.com, shippingsidekick.com

Turn off your computer – it helps to use a power strip and turn off your peripherals too.

Use a cooling base on your laptop – this extends the life of your laptop.

Use a smart power strip - these will shut down all your devices when you shut off the pc

Use online credit card processing - eliminate the swipe machine, the paper, the ink and the phone line use, use Squareup.com to process cards online and mobile.

Use open source software - like Open Office, and Gimp they are free and work just as well as the Microsoft and Adobe products.

FINANCIAL

Track your expenditures - once you see where your money is going you may rethink certain behaviors. MINT.com is a free app that works online and mobile and tracks your expenses against your accounts.

Avoid ATM fees - only withdraw cash from fee-less bank machines.

Avoid missed payments - fines and feeds add up.

Avoid submitting an insurance claim - it may not be worth the increase in premiums, ask your agent before you file

Buy index funds not mutual funds - , index funds will perform better overall and have no management fees.

Buy low cost mutual funds - this is easy to miss because the money doesn't come out of your pocket each month. But keep an eye on the cost of the mutual funds in your 401(k) and other investments. No fund should cost more than 1% and the combined cost for all your funds should be less than 0.50%.

Buy term life insurance – any other life insurance product is just not worth the extra cost.

Check your bills and receipts – always look for mistakes and double charges, it happens more frequently than we realize these days; save them in the car or in your bag so that you HAVE it to return to the store.

Consolidate your credit card debt – usually to a cheaper card, or using home equity to pay it off.

Do your own taxes, or not – if you have very simple taxes and forms do them yourself, if you don't, a professional may find you deductions you didn't know about.

Don't carry debt – pay your cards off before they raise your interest rate on your old debt.

Don't spend unexpected money – if you win the jackpot or get an inheritance, put the 'found' money away, since you didn't expect it anyway, you won't miss it. if you have to, put half towards outstanding bills and put the other half away.

Don't spend your change – collect the change from the couch and car, and periodically roll it and spend it on something particular.

Don't use a traditional IRA if you don't get the tax benefit – use a Roth IRA instead.

Don't use credit cards – if you can't pay it off in one or two months, it may not be economical to use your card for that purchase.

Don't carry your credit cards – buying on credit shouldn't be an impulse choice.

Don't print pages you don't have to – there is software on the market which combine multiple pages on one page; fineprint.com.

Don't pay for rewards programs you may not use – unless you buy a lot from a store or service, a paid membership may not be worth the expense

Avoid change conversion machines – the machines in the grocery store charge 8 or 9 cents on the dollar.

If you get a raise, bank the difference – add your raise to the amount you pay yourself every week, odds are you won't notice it gone from your paycheck.

Increase insurance deductibles – raising your deductibles gets you a better rate.

Keep grown kids on your health insurance policy – it is cheaper than having them pay for their own coverage; usually you can do this until they are 26.

Look for no fee accounts and debit cards – many banks have no fee accounts and debit cards.

Only take money out once a week – this is your weekly spending money.

Optimize your bank account – check to make sure you have the best account for your usage, one without fees, you shouldn't be paying to keep your money in their bank.

Pay bills online – many utilities and vendors give a discount when you eliminate the paper notice, some charge for the paper bills.

Pay local bills in cash – ask if there is a discount to paying in cash. Alas some local bills such as city bills and insurance can only be paid by check.

Avoid late fees by paying bills on time, use automatic debit, or set up a Google Calendar with email or text reminders of deadlines.

Pay car insurance, internet services, and life insurance annually – you will get a better rate than if you pay it monthly and save on interest.

Pay your mortgage twice a month instead of once – if your interest compounds based on the average monthly balance this will end up saving you money over time.

Pay yourself first – put way 10% of your income if you can, even if it is only ten dollars, put something aside from every check.

Put your savings into a money market instead of savings acct – money market has higher rates and yet are just as accessible.

Request a reduction in the interest rate on your credit cards – this works quite often, companies would rather you stay with them, then pay interest elsewhere.

Reserve your credit card for emergencies – after you have cut up all but one card, put that one in your dresser and save it for emergencies.

Save one months living expenses – and when that's done, put away 3 months living expenses.

Set up a Non Wage-Earning Spousal IRA – the spouse of a stay-at-home spouse that is eligible to set up an Individual Retirement Account can set up a Non Wage-Earning Spousal IRA, up to the qualified amount ($5000 per person this year and an additional $1000 if you are over 50).

Take advantage of employer 401(k) matches – if your employer matches 401(k) contributions, do everything you can to take full advantage of that match.

Use and track rebates – many companies aren't diligent about sending you your rebate, keep copies and mark it on your calendar to follow up.

Use debit cards instead - pay yourself first, by putting money into a debit card to use instead of a credit card, that way you are borrowing from yourself.

Use flexible spending accounts - FSAs allow you to pay certain medical, dental and child care expenses using pre-tax dollars.

Use local banks - local banks are more accommodating than national banks; private banks also have less restrictive rules.

TRANSPORTATION

Sell your vehicle - if you live in a city you may only need to rent a car several times a year. If you have a garage you can rent it out.

Avoid using A/C - if you can drive with the window down do so, on the highway this may cause drag, set the A/C to low and the fan to high.

Avoid short or pointless errands - do the math, see how much it costs you to go a mile, traveling to save small amounts isn't economically sound.

Bicycle when you can - this saves wear and tear on your vehicle, saves gas, improves your health.

Buy regular gas - if you car MUST have high-grade gasoline, you are probably driving too much car.

Buy things you can wash - an awful lot of things sold in pet stores aren't washing machine friendly, a pet bed that can't be laundered has a short life span.

Carpool - split the wear between your vehicle and others.

Car sharing - split car ownership with a close friend.

Clean your vehicle's air filter - this improves efficiency.

Combine errands – this saves gas and wear on your vehicle.

Do you own oil change – encourages you to keep your car tuned.

Do your own maintenance – the more familiar you are with your own vehicle, the better you will care for it and the longer it will last.

Don't use the dealership for oil changes – use your local guy or do it yourself it's not rocket science.

Drive at non-peak times – don't fight traffic, idling in traffic just wastes gas and makes you angry.

Fill your car up when you're down to a quarter tank of gas. You won't be stuck going to the nearest, most expensive gas station when your car is on empty.

Get tires from wholesale clubs – they are significantly cheaper there. If you know you will be needing them keep an eye out for sales, coupons and deals which include free install; even if you put them off before the last ones are completely 'gone'.

Keep maintenance records and receipts – if you had something fixed and it needs fixing again, it was probably not fixed right the first time.

Keep tires properly inflated – this keeps you safe and costs less on gas.

Keep your car longer – avoid the urge to trade in or up for as long as you can.

Keep your vehicle tuned up – if you vehicle runs as it should, it will save gas oil and maintenance charges.

Remove excess weight – your vehicle will use less gas without all the stuff in your trunk.

Shop around for gas – websites compare gasoline prices in your neighborhood; gasbuddy.com.

Shop for a local repair shop – check consumer reviews online, make sure it's ASE-certified and get recommendations.

Shop for car insurance – if you aren't in a highly regulated state, you may get a better rate.

Trade down – you don't need a luxury vehicle, or an off road vehicle for city driving and commuting.

Travel with your pet – instead of boarding it this time, look for places that welcome pets.

Use a discount card to buy gas. (Many grocery stores offer them, as well as Costco).

Use cruise control on highways – this will save gas.

Use public transportation – saves wear and tear on your own vehicle.

Walk when you can – this saves wear and tear on your vehicle, saves gas, improves your health.

Wash your own car – a clean car lasts longer, especially where roads are salted. Simply washing and rinsing your own car takes less than a half hour; improves resale value.

Share your vehicle, split the maintenance costs with a neighbor or friend, in exchange for use.

Hire your vehicle and yourself out on craigslist to help people move or drive them on errands and shopping.

Car pool – yes this is a very old concept, but just as frugal; because of varying schedules you may only do it a few days a week or month, but each day you don't drive your vehicle saves you money, and for the most part driving two people doesn't cost that much more than one.

Don't break the law – speeding and other ticketable expenses can be avoided.

TRAVEL

To go bag – have an overnight bag ready with airline appropriate sized containers and supplies, you won't have to buy new ones at the last minute

Take mini vacations- a weekend here and there can be rejuvenating, even if you camp in your car or a tent. 24 hour overnight bike trips are popular. Leave on the Saturday morning, get to your camp site, come back on Sunday. It can be immensely satisfying to get away.

Staycation – for those who commute this may actually be a joy, just don't tell anyone you are at home that week. You can use the occasion to do day trips within driving distance.

Carry food on trips – avoid buying food when you are in your car or traveling, bring snacks and sandwiches with you. Bring a refillable water container and a small cooler from a yard sale.

Travel Light – Airlines charge for everything now and if you have a bag, expect to be charged for it. Remember to not use over sized bags whenever possible and try to keep it all within one bag per person.

Travel in the off season – when prices are cheaper.

Use the Mail – If you acquire 'stuff' consider shipping it all back. The larger USPS shipping box is cheaper than a second baggage fee. You can always pack your new stuff and ship back your laundry.

Check on the round trip. – sometimes the round trip ticket is cheaper than a one way. I am not kidding about that. If you find a cheaper one, just don't use the other half of the ticket.

Just Drive – If you add up the ticket and the car rental, it may be cheaper to just drive.

Eat in – Bring a soft squishable cooler and start collecting food for your hotel room. Extra rolls from dinner; fruit, biscuits, yogurts from the nearest market. Whatever you can gather up while you are out and about. The ice in the hotel room is free after all.

Drink in – Bring a manual drip coffee filter and or an immersion water heater. Collect Sugar and creams from the restaurant, have your own coffee or tea in your room.

PETS

Adopt from shelters – this helps ensure you will get a well and happy pet, pet store pets are notoriously unwell and short lived; shelters will even take the pet back and keep it safe should you need it.

Avoid buying pet 'furniture' – completely unnecessary, cats like wicker chairs and hampers as much as a scratching post, old crib mattresses make great dog beds, old bus pans from restaurants make swell litter pans.

Buy cat litter at the feed store – They will have many brands in bags and boxes, but some corn based chicken feeds can be used as cat litter and are even cheaper.

Buy dry pet food at the feed store – 50 pound bags are much cheaper than the 10 pound bags at the grocery store.

Buy flea/tick treatments online – flea, tick and regular treatments are cheaper online.

Buy food in bulk – obviously the smaller packages the higher the unit price.

Buy heartworm medications online – many things are much cheaper online.

Buy soft toys at yard sales – toys made for very small children are quite safe.

Don't buy cheap pet food – avoids illnesses and improves health; stick to 'better' brands, ask your vet or the pet store to compare them for you.

Don't overfeed – we know you love your pets, your pet knows you love it, food is not love; an overweight animal has a shorter lifespan and is prone to illnesses such as diabetes and arthritis just like humans.

Find an older veterinarian – older vets have been out of school for years and may not have the expenses such as school loans that younger veterinarians do.

Find a veterinary school – the students are overseen by their instructors.

Foster pets for your local shelter – allows you to test drive the idea of having a pet, the shelter will cover the food and medical bills.

Groom your pet at home – as long as you don't need a show cut, and your pet isn't overly anxious, this can save you a lot of money; an electric shaver may pay for itself in one session.

Keep your cat inside – this eliminates the chance of injury or illness.

Keep your dog inside your yard – use a visible or invisible fence, this will reduce the changes of injury or illness.

Make play dates – this keeps your pet healthy not just happy.

Stretch heartworm meds – the FDA found that Heartguard, Interceptor and Revolution provide protection beyond the 30 days; the 30 days schedule was recommend to help you remember when to do it, so dosing your dog every 30-45 days will stretch your dogs dosage schedule.

Train your dog well – if your dog is not properly socialized, it can become skittish and fearful, biting the mailman, visitors, children or small animals is costly and may cost your dog its freedom or life.

Use clinics for vaccinations – Pet stores and shelters hold these on a regular basis, eliminates the vet office visit fee.

Walk your own dog – not only keeps your pet happy but improves your health.

YARD

Eliminate the grass – replace some or all of your lawn with native and low water using plants.

Save rain water – this can be illegal in some places, but a simple diverter for your gutters can provide water for your garden and other outdoor chores.

Start a garden – start small with a few plants you know you can tend to, high yield low maintenance like tomatoes and squashes, if it works out plant more next year, gradually increase the size each year.

Container garden –If you don't have sunny space to plant, or any exposed dirt at all. You can still container garden on a fire escape, patio, window sill or stair case. Recycle the soil by dumping it all into a large bin a the end of the season, add more mulch and potting soil, stir it up and let it compost in the dark until next season.

Grow herbs in aquariums – use a large glass fish tank with a top light to protect your herbs over winter or all year long if you don't have a yard. Don't forget to put a timer on the light that approximates sunlight exposure.

Trade seedlings – join the garden club or offer to trade seedlings on the local bulletin board.

Plant perennials – It's always best when you don't' have to replant every year.

Save your own seeds – let some of your flowers and vegetables go to seed. Save and dry the seeds for next year.

Grow local varieties.– don't try to force plants to grow that aren't suited to your climate. Find Seed catalogs produced in your zone and close to your house as possible. Pick exciting heritage varieties that were once grown in your town. These unusual varieties are much more desirable to barter and usually hardier.

Check for free stuff from your town – your local dump may have free mulch or firewood. Even if they have bagged leaves you can use it as a starter for your mulch pile.

Find a local farmer or horse barn – they Always have manure, the problem is everyone wants it. Offer to barter some produce for access to the mulch.

Try hay for mulch and weed killer – spreading the straw or salt marsh hay under your plants against the ground like a carpet will smother weeds and keep the ground warm and damp. It also makes a great cushion for any fruits and vegetables that grown near the ground.

Reduce Recycle and Reuse

Recycle whatever you can – especially when you pay for your trash removal.

Swap or sell books, DVDs and CDs you no longer need – if they aren't worth enough to swap or sell, donate them and get the space in your house back.

Watch the trash – see what people throw away and understand the ephemeral nature of many purchases; more particle-board computer desks are on curbs than in bedrooms, small outdoor grills never get cleaned properly left in the rain and tossed out, box fans covered in cat hair get pitched instead of a yearly cleaning.

Watch the trash - better neighborhoods throw better things. You may not want to put that piece of furniture in your house, but you can sell it on craigslist or at a yard sale. Even putting things on freecycle earns you credit as a GIVER not just someone who wants things.

Reduce the number of toys – exchange or donate toys that aren't being played with, this will eliminate clutter and keep other toys from getting broken in storage

Reusable items for children's parties – non disposable plastic plates and cups washed and saved for repeated use; washing takes energy but it is less than repurchasing each time.

Switch to cloth napkins at home – these are especially cheap at thrift stores or restaurant supply houses and will last for decades.

Use dishtowels and cleaning rags - this will cut down on paper towel use, reserving paper towels for the kind of stuff you really don't want in the laundry. Cleaning rags come in packets of 48, 50, or 60 etc.

Trade toys - host a toy party where kids bring good toys that they're willing to exchange.

Use generic wrapping paper for all occasions - vary the ribbon or decoration, hand decorate single colored paper.

Reuse sheets and towels - into pillowcases and cleaning rags.

Use white open stock dinnerware - it will all match and you can add serving and replacement pieces from the thrift store easily.

Don't save scrap materials for potential projects longer than a reasonable time - if you don't use cardboard tubes, boxes and scrap materials within a month, toss them you can always get more. Saving trash to reuse in projects you weren't going to do anyway is false economy

Decorate with natural items - if you decorate with greenery and items from nature they can go into the compost bin afterwards.

Eliminate seasonal redecorating - don't buy new house decorations every season, go through ones in storage and reuse them or give up seasonal specific changes; trade old decorations with a friend.

Mat and frame your own photographs as artwork. You will get many compliments and may have a chance of selling copies.

Mail things back to the maker - If you can't return them to place of purchase send devices and products that disappoint you back to their original manufacturer.

Find the address of the parent company, President or Vice President in charge of something. This can be pricey if you are shipping back a hand held vacuum or blender or such. But generally they will repair it or send a coupon or call you. The worst that happens is nothing, but that is the rarity.

DECLUTTER

Clean your house – Less clutter improves atmosphere and mental health. An uncluttered house tends to be easier to keep clean and use less energy to heat and cool, since there is easier air circulation.

Avoid dead storage – each cubic foot costs in rent or mortgage, unused items are using that money.

Get rid of off site storage – if you haven't used something in 6 months to a year you don't need it. If you use it less frequently you can rent it cheaper than you can store it. If you can store those things for free at a friends house do it, especially useful for items you can share like canoes.

Stop collecting things – collections demand attention, stop buying collectibles, and other commemorative items.

Sell or give away extra things – unused items can be converted to cash and take up space better used for other things.

Look for competitive rates for trash removal – sometimes you can get a better offer, ask your service to match it.

Break things down. Break down large objects into pieces that fit in trash bags and bins to avoid paying extra for its removal.

Dispose of trash elsewhere. If you live someplace where large items cost extra to throw out. check with your relatives in other towns, if it costs less or is free, ask if you can put it in their trash the night before pick up.

Earning Extra

Don't invest money you can't afford to loose. Build micro-income sources slowly, take money from cans and bottles and buy thrift store items for resale.

Baby sit – even if for an hour so that someone can go grocery shopping, it is a valuable service.

Become a mystery shopper – mysteryshop.org.

Busk – perform, mime, juggle, break dance, be a statue, play any instrument, spoons, the harmonica etc...find a public space to set up in on a regular basis during peak hours, people don't appreciate it if they are trying to sleep and you are under their window. Check to see if you need a local permit.

Buy second hand clothing for resale – many 'name' items can be resold for more money, especially if they have their original labels and tags.

Check out online selling sites – instead of Ebay.com and Amazon.com, try free listing sites where the low fee come out of the sale, like Bonanza.com and Biblio.com.

Clean and detail other people's cars – the simple act of vacuuming their car may be beyond many people.

Clean out basements and garages – most of it will be trash, so you will have to factor in the cost of a trip to the dump, but some items may be salable on Craigslist.com or yard sales, if they don't sell put them on freecycle.com.

Collect and sell old cell phones –recellular.com, usell.com.

Collect cans and bottles - there are ways to do this surreptitiously, merely walking around town or your neighborhood with a knapsack would yield a dollar or two.

Cruise trash days for resalable items - either the night before or the morning of trash pick up, don't forget weekend post yard sale afternoons.

Do outdoor chores - not just the elderly need leaves raked, fallen branches picked up, storm windows raised, a/c units put in windows, weeds pulled from walkways, tires moved from the trunk to the basement etc.

Donate plasma - some places pay for plasma and rare blood types.

Elder sit - home caregivers are desperate for personal time, they may not be able to pay generously, but they will reciprocate or compensate you in other ways; getting professional references makes it easier.

Enter contests with your crafts and recipes - there are actual cash prizes to be won, sell the non cash prizes. Contestbee.com

Get a paper route -carriers are always coming and going, and news paper distributors always seem to need help; the pay isn't much and the hours are early (and short) but it is something, and may work well around mothers hours.

Get paid for medical experiments - more often then not they are just taking medications for ailments you already have and recording the reactions.

Grow to sell - pick a crop you like and are good at and grow much more than you will ever use, swap the excess other growers or sell it at a local farmers market.

Have a garage/yard sale - collect things for months ahead, be very organized, start high and slowly reduce prices, they sell everything cheap - have nothing left.

House sit – either live-in or as a constant caretaker an empty home is a target and this is always a needed service.

Learn a specific repair skill – repair bicycles, jewelry, leather goods, books, eyeglasses, fix computers, lawnmower, etc.; very specific desirable skills can always be traded for goods or money.

Lend tools or service – if you have a chain saw, offer to cut whatever needs cutting for a fee, it is safer than lending it to someone who doesn't have one.

Look for an online job – freelance online writing, website design, call centers, research, sales all of these can be done from the home. Check Craigslist. Fiverr.com allows you to post jobs that you will do for $5.

Look for storage container auctions - much of the contents will have to be taken to the dump at your expense, but you can make a profit if you keep at it and get more skilled at reselling the items.

Pet sit, long term – military personnel on assignment and families following a parent working outside the country want their pets cared for and will pay the expenses and more to have it done. Check with local shelters and vets for referrals.

Pet sit, short term – many folks just need someone to feed their cats while they are away or take their dog for a quick weekend jaunt.

Rent out a room – if you live near a city or a college, you can usually find a transfer student or teacher who needs a place to stay. In summer you can find seasonal travelers and exchange students.

Rent storage space – in your garage or on your property, just be careful about liability for loss or damage.

Sell clothing on consignment – if you have expensive designer or handmade clothing, a consignment shop may be your best option.

Sell extra media: DVDs and CDs – check the prices on Ebay.com before you list. They may be a glut on the market and you may get immediate cash for a reduced amount at a local vendor.

Sell furniture on consignment – consignment may not be as easy as selling on Craiglist.com or ebay.com, it depends on the item's desirability and sometimes the size and the location of the store.

Sell something unique on the internet – one item specific to you, something common that has been personalized or a some small device or kit made of assembled parts; any small amount of sales is better than nothing.

Sell your china and crystal to a replacement company – some piece are more common than others, hollowware, things with lids and handles are more desirable; replacements.com.

Sell your crafts – whether sewn, knitted, woodwork, metalwork, if your hobby can pay for itself; etsy.com.

Sell your eggs to fertility clinics or sperm to a sperm bank – depending on where you live and your overall health this may be an option.

Sell your hair to a wigmaker – if your hair is long and untreated it can be very desirable.

Sell your photos as stock photos – uploading to a photo bank can be free of fees; iStockphoto.com, BigStockPhoto, Shutterstock.

Start a blog – even marginally popular blogs can make money from embedded advertisements through different online programs. the more specific the theme of the blog the easier it will be for visitors to find you; see google.com/adsense, adsensealternatives.org.

Start an errand service – many people with straight jobs need things done during the week, dogs walked, meds picked up, dry cleaning, shopping, not just seniors.

Teach basic computer skills – advertise on Craigslist.com or locally to teach people in their home basic computer skills: MS Word, Excel, Facebook, Blogger, Wordpress; you will be surprised at how many people aren't as tech savvy as yourself.

Trade services – if you are a mechanic and your friend is an accountant an exchange of services can be quite fair, however be resolved not to trade DOWN.

Tutor – if you have a degree or other specialty, tutor high school or college students.

Write a book – Find a subject that you love and want to share with the public. Self publishing with an internet print on demand site, such as CreateSpace.com and Blurb.com has nearly no investment costs. Digital publishing such as Smashwords.com and Amazon's Kindle Direct Publishing have no set up costs.

ABOUT THE AUTHOR.

J. Godsey is an editor, ghost-writer and publisher with SicPress.com. Volunteers many years with Animal Rescue Veterinary Services, Londonderry, NH, Animal Rescue Merrimack Valley, The Wolf Adventure, Goffstown, NH, Methuen Rail Trail Alliance, Methuen Trails Committee, Community Emergency Response Teams. For the last 30 years has been researching and practicing an extremely frugal lifestyle.

Please review this book.

If you have any suggestions for inclusion please contact sales@sicpress.com

Your purchase goes towards animal rescue care and rehabilitation.

www.ingramcontent.com/pod-product-compliance
Lightning Source LLC
Chambersburg PA
CBHW050539210326
41520CB00012B/2644